I CAN DRAW
PEOPLE

I CAN DRAW
PEOPLE
BY GILL SPEIRS

A LITTLE SIMON BOOK
PUBLISHED BY SIMON & SCHUSTER, INC., NEW YORK

HERE'S HOW

I CAN DRAW PEOPLE will show you, in easy-to-follow steps, how to recognize the simple shapes which build onto each other to make up a person.

Before you start to draw from the easy instructions in the book, get to know what your pen or pencil will do.

Use a large sheet of paper and draw all over it with large, bold strokes. Use all the space you have on your paper and try to make all your lines free and flowing. This will give you confidence.

Read the section GETTING STARTED and experiment with the different textures it shows.

I CAN DRAW PEOPLE will teach you how to draw boys and girls, men and women, running, jumping and standing still – but don't rush! Follow the step-by-step guides to first learn how the basic shapes fit together to form a balanced figure.

Most important of all, you must practice. Draw as often as you can and you will soon develop the skill to draw people in any situation.

Make up the little action figure given on the back cover. You can pose it in all sorts of positions and use it as a model for your drawings.

GETTING STARTED

Remember two very important points when you first start to draw. You must use your eyes all the time to search out the basic shapes and forms of all you see. Learn how they underline everything that you draw. You must practice. This is the only way to get to know your subject really well.

Keep your pencil moving freely and don't be afraid of making mistakes. They are part of learning too!

Pencils, crayons and pens can all be used to draw with.

PENCILS are clean and easy to use. They can be soft or hard or in between. An "H" pencil will give a hard, crisp line and a "B" a soft gentle line. An "HB" pencil is nice to start with as a good point will draw sharp lines. Used on its side, the point will give you soft textures as well.

HARCOAL gives a soft, black line.
harcoal bought in pencil form
; easiest to use and less messy.
harcoal can be smudged for
ood shading, but take care
ot to smudge everything!

ASTELS need the same care
s charcoal and can be bought
n many different colors.

ENS of every sort are available,
or thick lines and thin. The best
nd cheapest kind are fiber or
lt tip pens. You can choose from
ots of colors and widths.

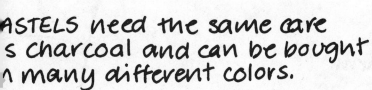
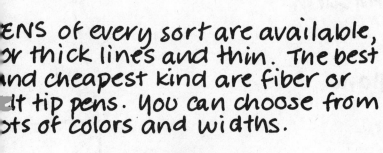

PARTS OF THE BODY

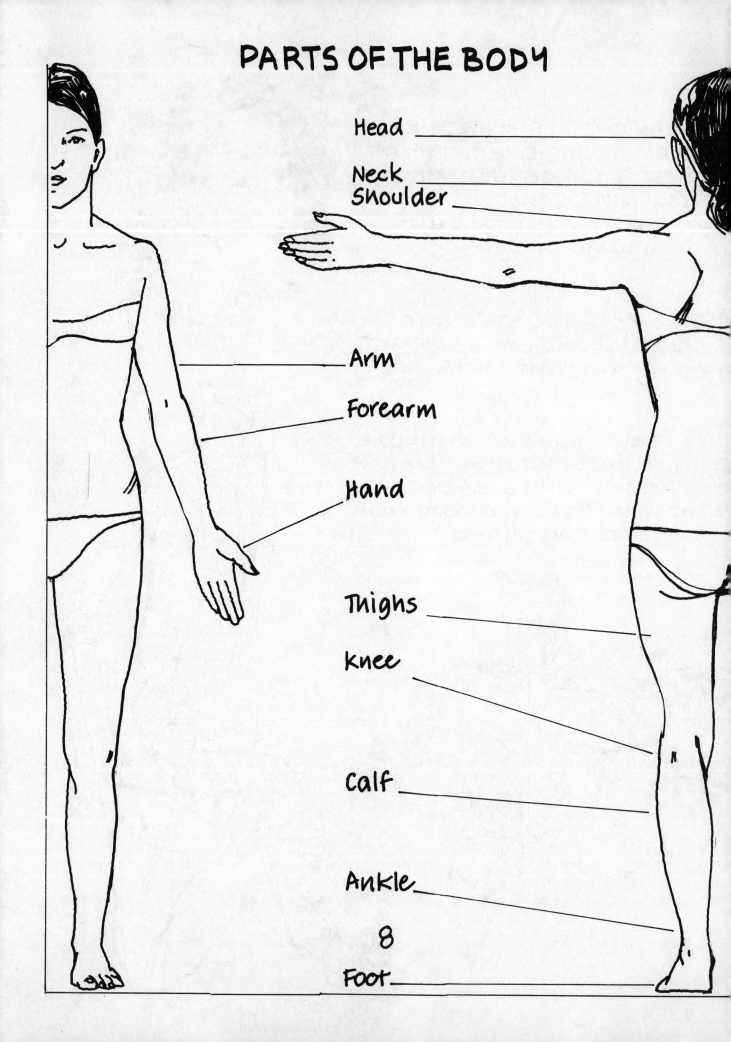

Head _____

Neck _____
Shoulder _____

Arm _____

Forearm _____

Hand _____

Thighs _____

Knee _____

Calf _____

Ankle _____

8

Foot _____

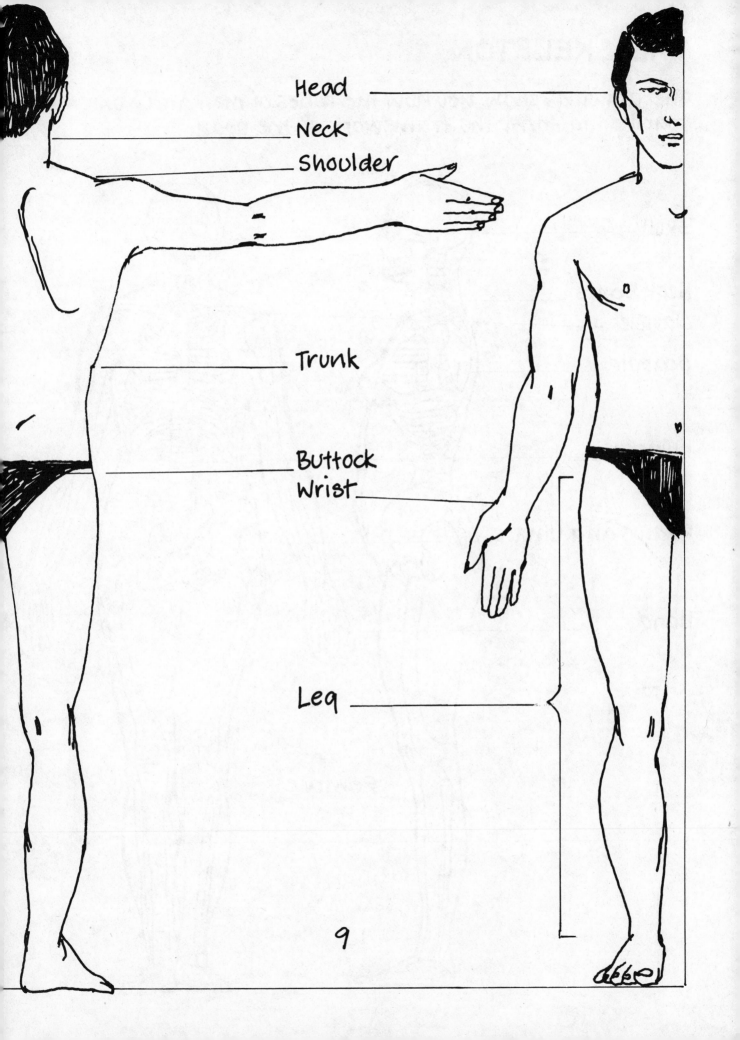

Head ————————————

Neck ————————————

Shoulder ————

Trunk

Buttock

Wrist————

Leg ————————————

9

THE SKELETON

The drawings show you how the bones of men and women join together to form the framework of the body.

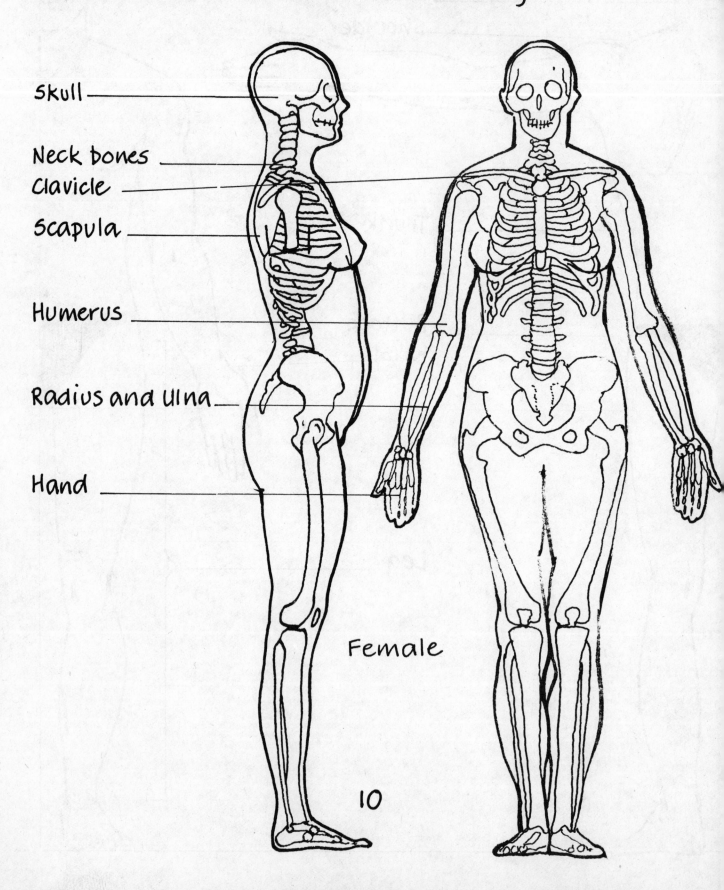

Skull

Neck bones

Clavicle

Scapula

Humerus

Radius and Ulna

Hand

Female

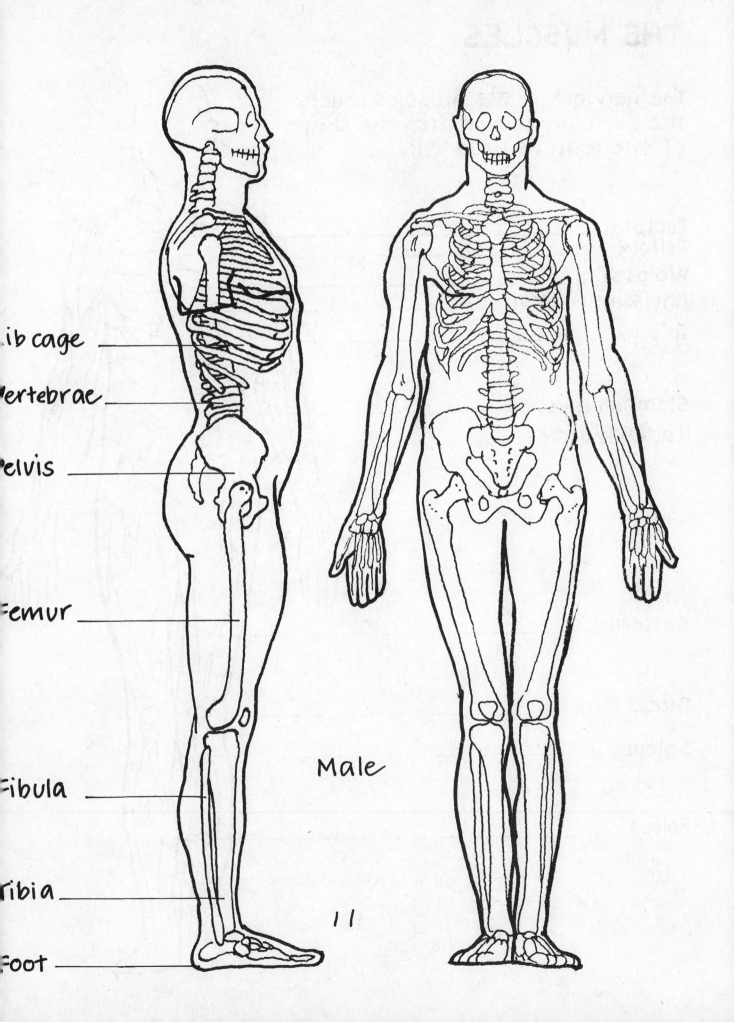

Rib cage _____

Vertebrae _____

Pelvis _____

Femur _____

Fibula _____

Tibia _____

Foot _____

Male

11

THE MUSCLES

The network of the muscles covers the skeleton and creates the shape of the body as you see it.

Pectoral _____

Deltoid _____

Biceps _____

Latissimus dorsi _____

Triceps _____

Stomach muscles _____

Radial muscles _____

Sartorius _____

Biceps femoris _____

Soleus _____

Soleus _____

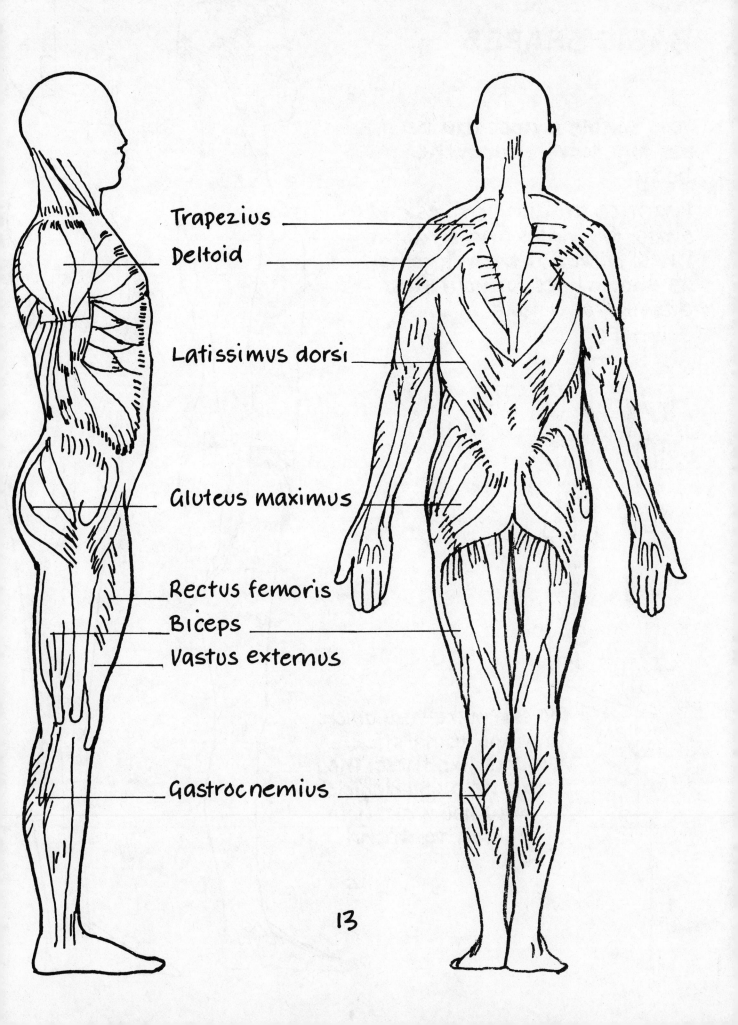

Trapezius

Deltoid

Latissimus dorsi

Gluteus maximus

Rectus femoris

Biceps

Vastus externus

Gastrocnemius

13

BASIC SHAPES

Very simple shapes can be put together to form the body.

Practice drawing circles and ovals, triangles and straight lines then put them together as shown here for your first drawing of a man.

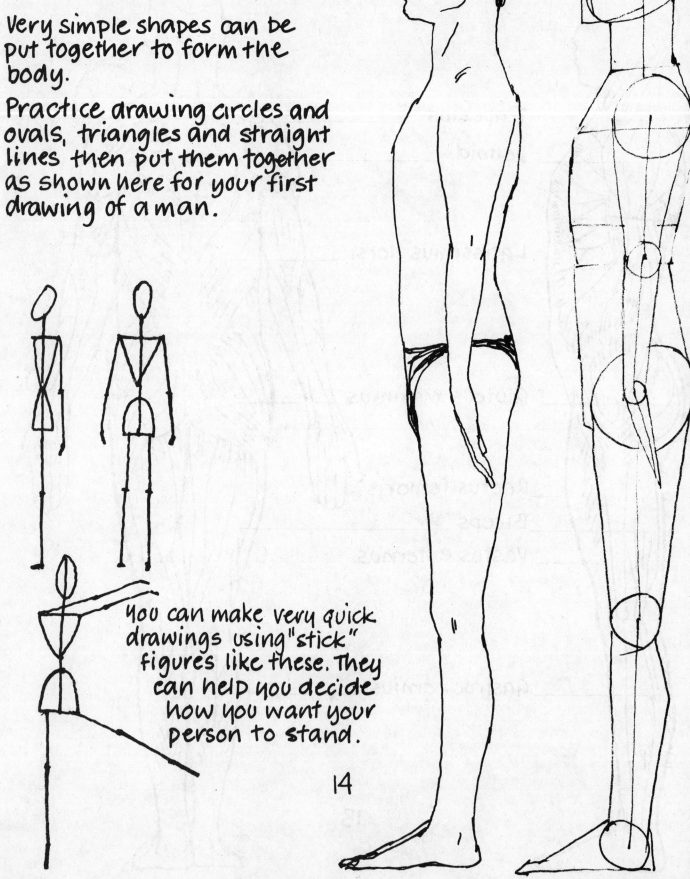

You can make very quick drawings using "stick" figures like these. They can help you decide how you want your person to stand.

14

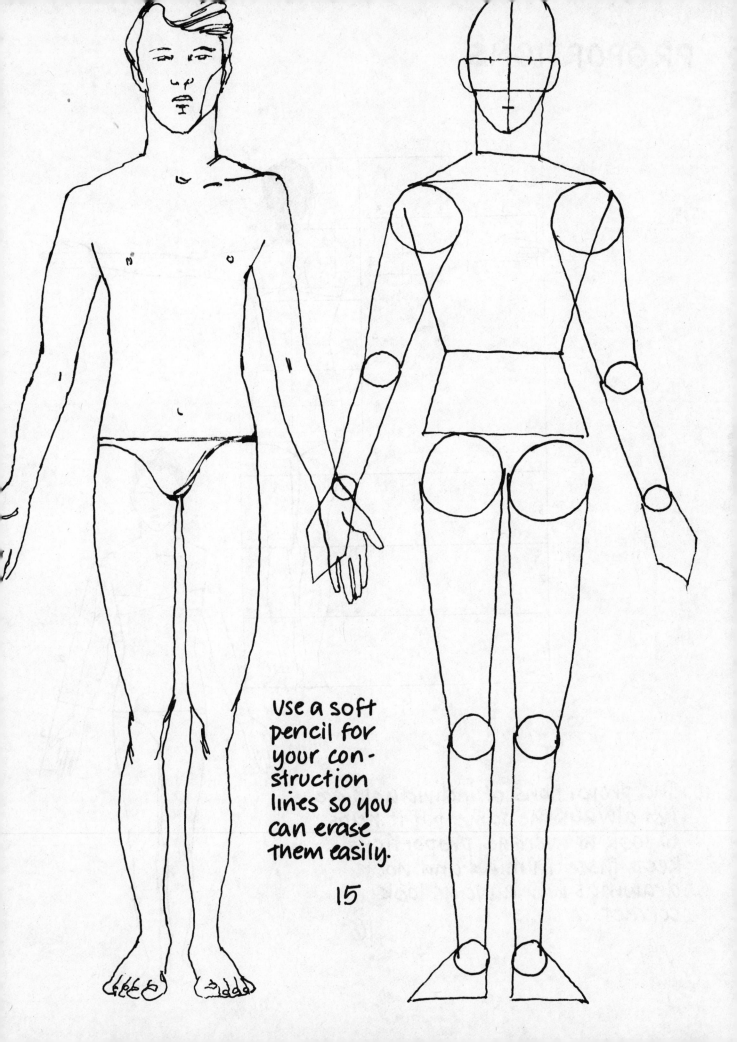

Use a soft
pencil for
your con-
struction
lines so you
can erase
them easily.

15

PROPORTIONS

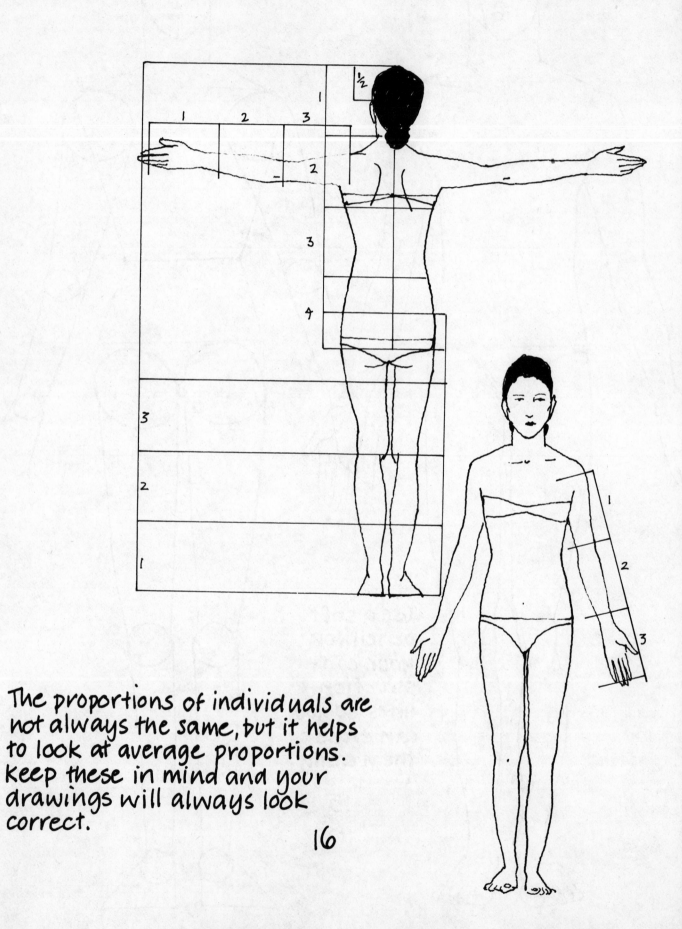

The proportions of individuals are not always the same, but it helps to look at average proportions. Keep these in mind and your drawings will always look correct.

16

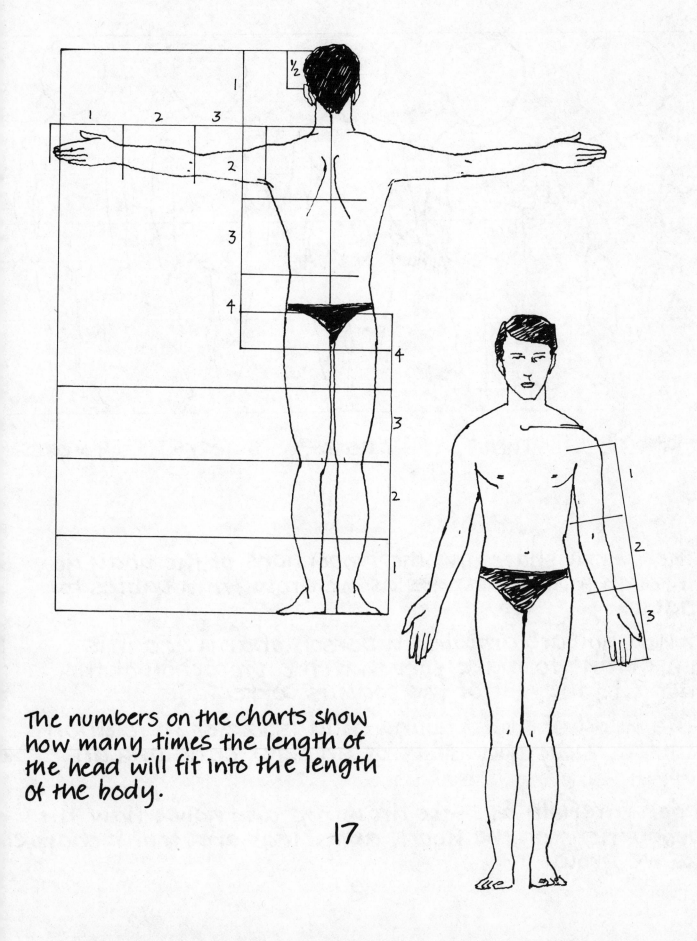

The numbers on the charts show
how many times the length of
the head will fit into the length
of the body.

17

PROPORTIONS — GROWING UP

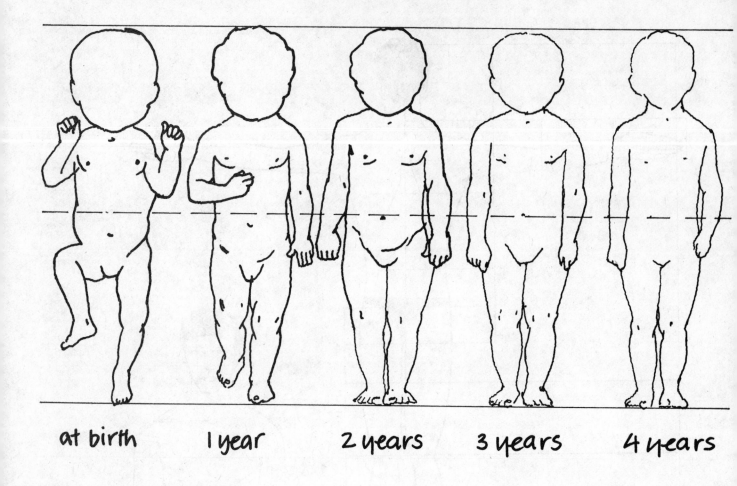

at birth   1 year   2 years   3 years   4 years

The overall shape and the proportions of the body go through many changes as we grow from babies to adults.

When you are drawing a person of any age it is important to make sure that the proportion of the head to the rest of the body is correct.

The head of a very young child is larger in relation to the body than that of an older child and an adult.

Look carefully at these drawings and notice how the proportions of the head, arms, legs and trunk change as we grow.

18

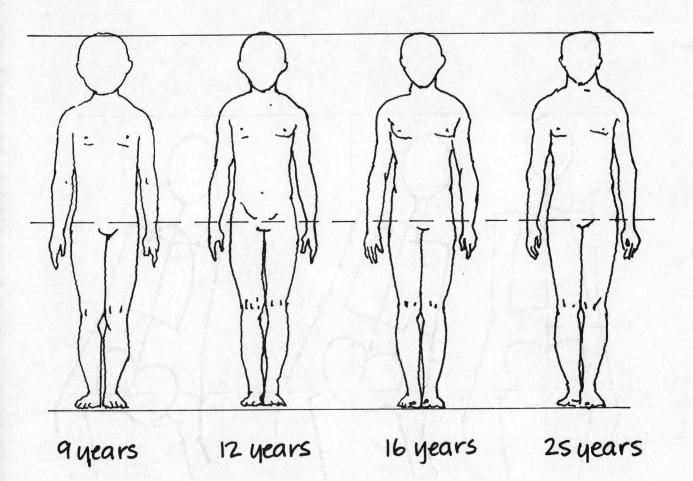

9 years   12 years   16 years   25 years

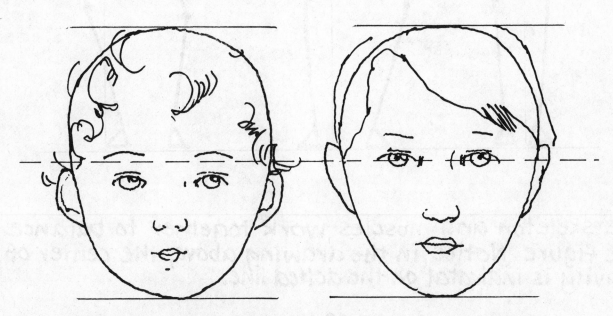

See how the proportions of the face also
change as we grow older.

BALANCE

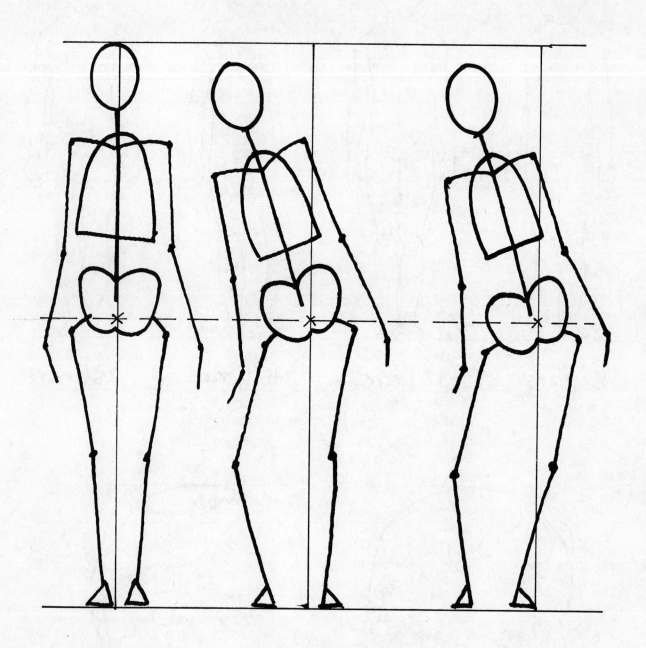

The skeleton and muscles work together to balance the figure. Notice, in the drawing above, the center of gravity is indicated on the dotted line.

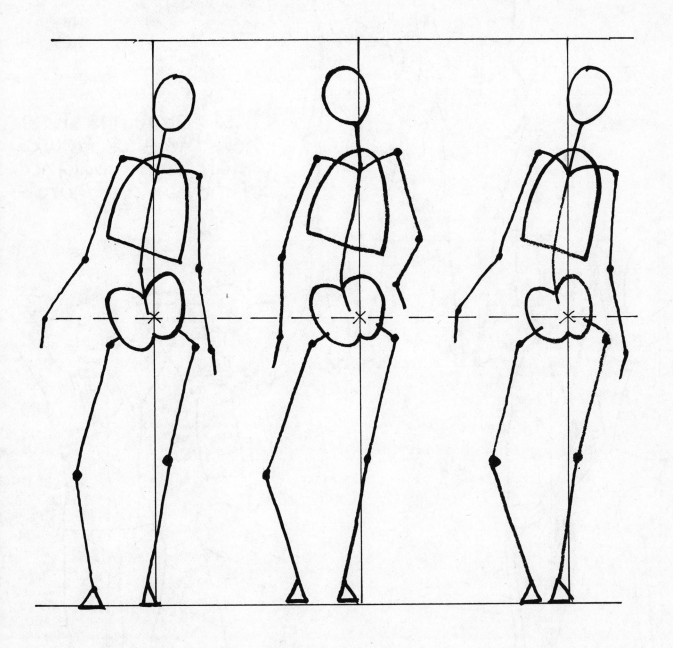

These simple stick figure drawings show how the body adjusts itself to stay upright when the position of the legs is changed.

21

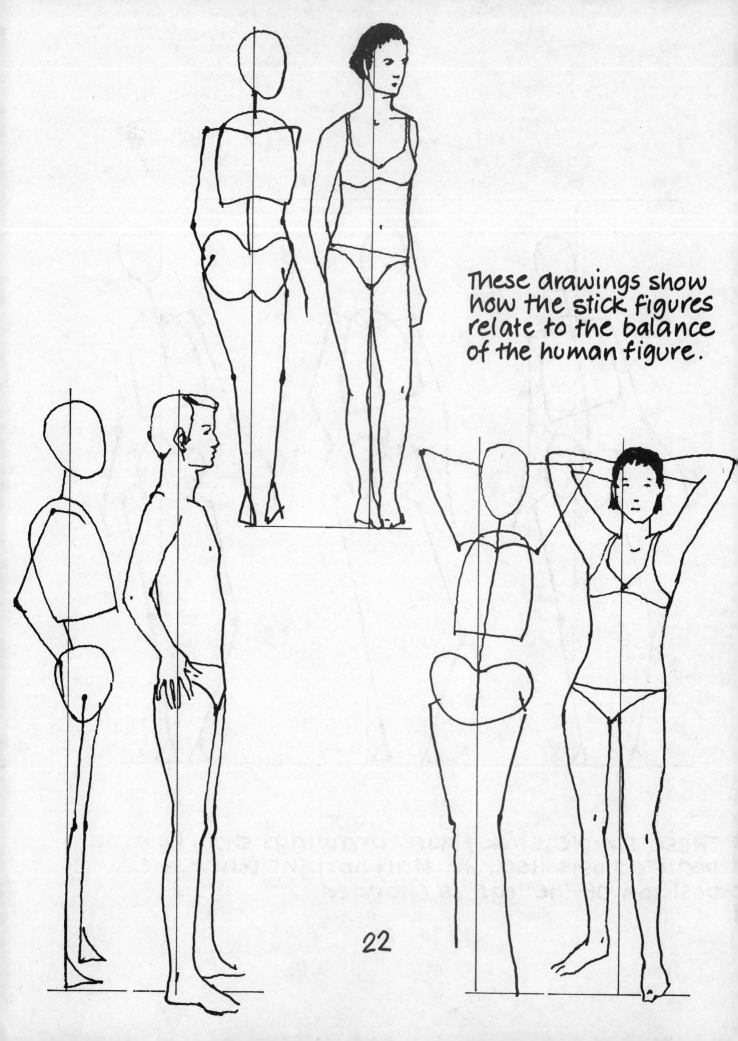

These drawings show
how the stick figures
relate to the balance
of the human figure.

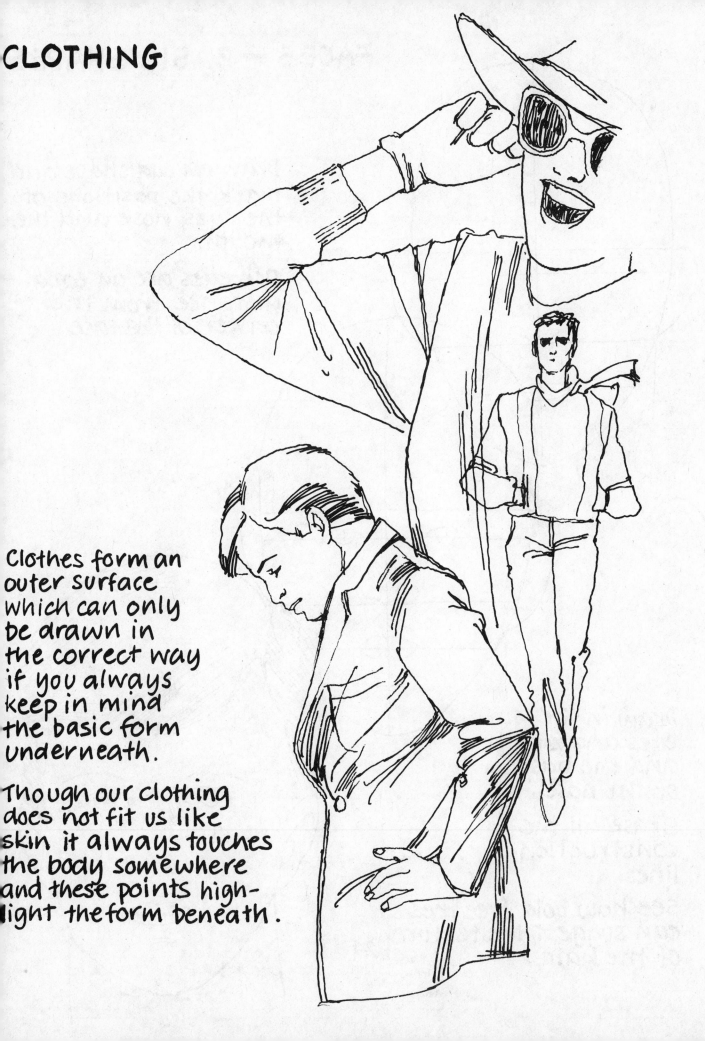

CLOTHING

Clothes form an
outer surface
which can only
be drawn in
the correct way
if you always
keep in mind
the basic form
underneath.

Though our clothing
does not fit us like
skin it always touches
the body somewhere
and these points high-
light the form beneath.

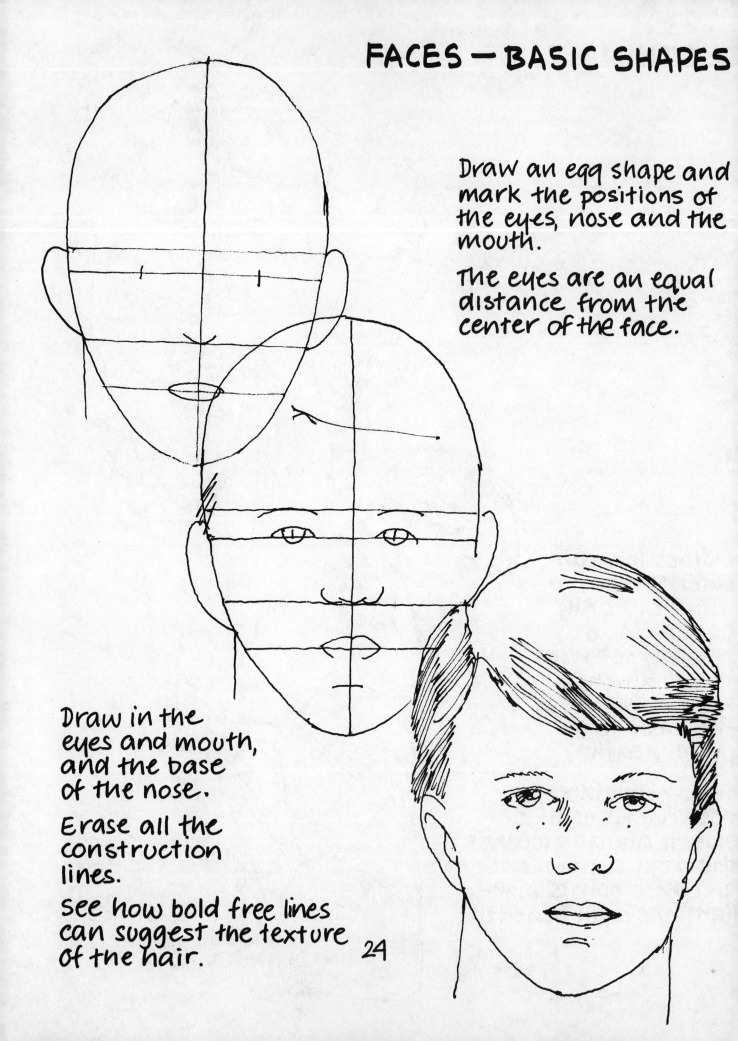

FACES — BASIC SHAPES

Draw an egg shape and mark the positions of the eyes, nose and the mouth.

The eyes are an equal distance from the center of the face.

Draw in the eyes and mouth, and the base of the nose.

Erase all the construction lines.

See how bold free lines can suggest the texture of the hair.

24

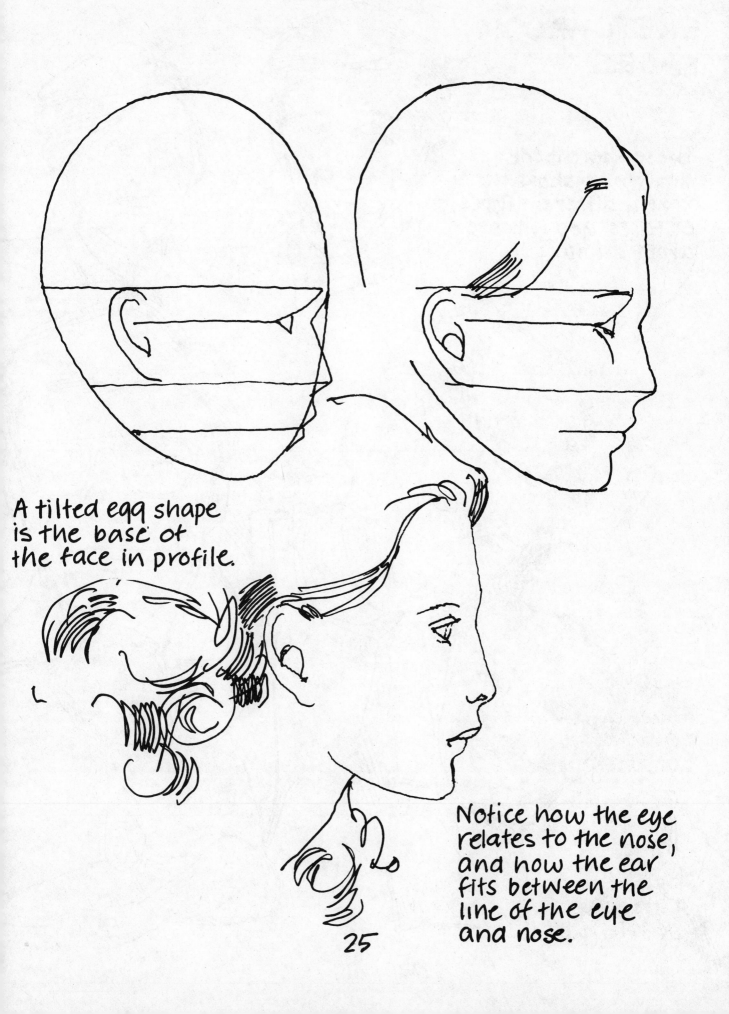

A tilted egg shape is the base of the face in profile.

Notice how the eye relates to the nose, and how the ear fits between the line of the eye and nose.

25

SKETCHBOOK FACES

These sketchbook drawings show the many different types of faces you will see around you.

HANDS—

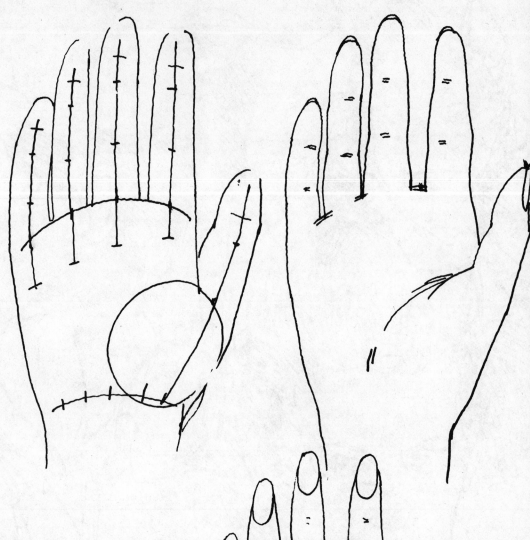

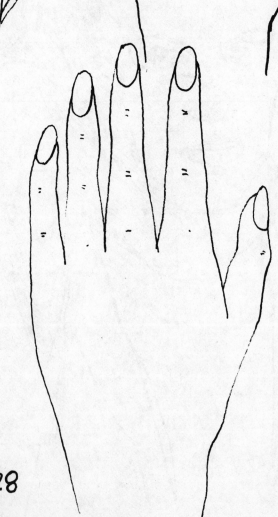

The hands are a very complicated part of the body, made up of lots of tiny bones and muscles.

But don't be afraid of drawing them too.

Break the hand in to basic shapes as here and you will find it much easier to draw.

28

BASIC SHAPES

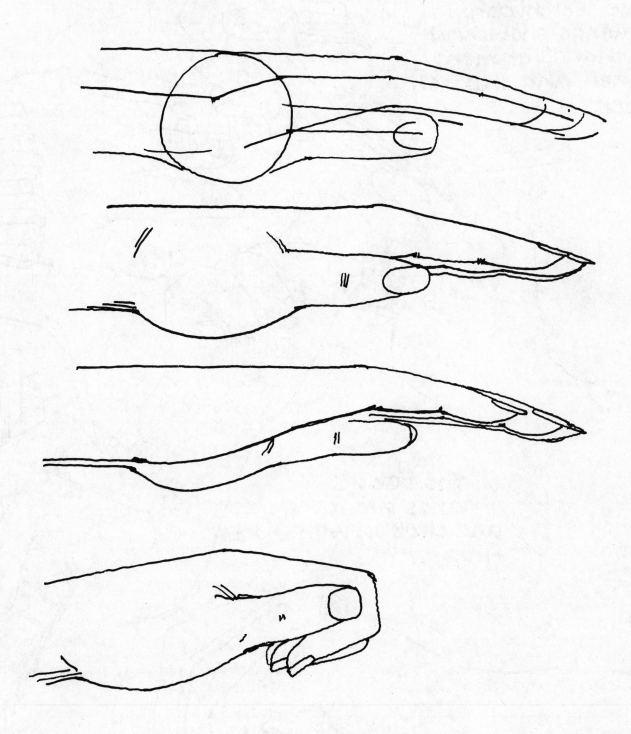

SKETCHBOOK HANDS

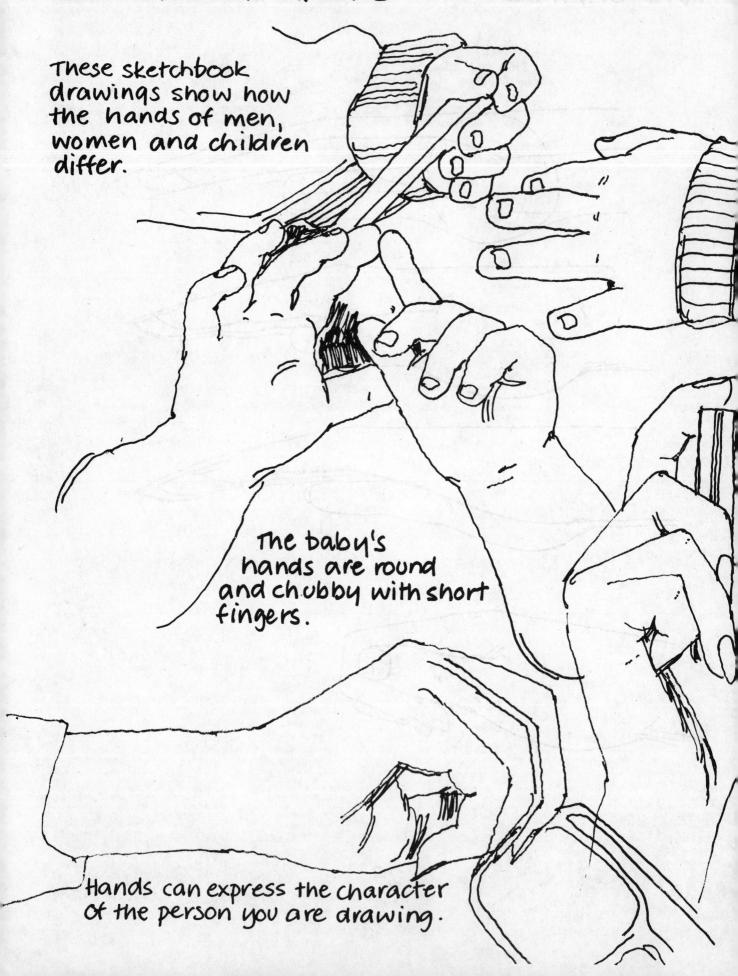

These sketchbook drawings show how the hands of men, women and children differ.

The baby's hands are round and chubby with short fingers.

Hands can express the character of the person you are drawing.

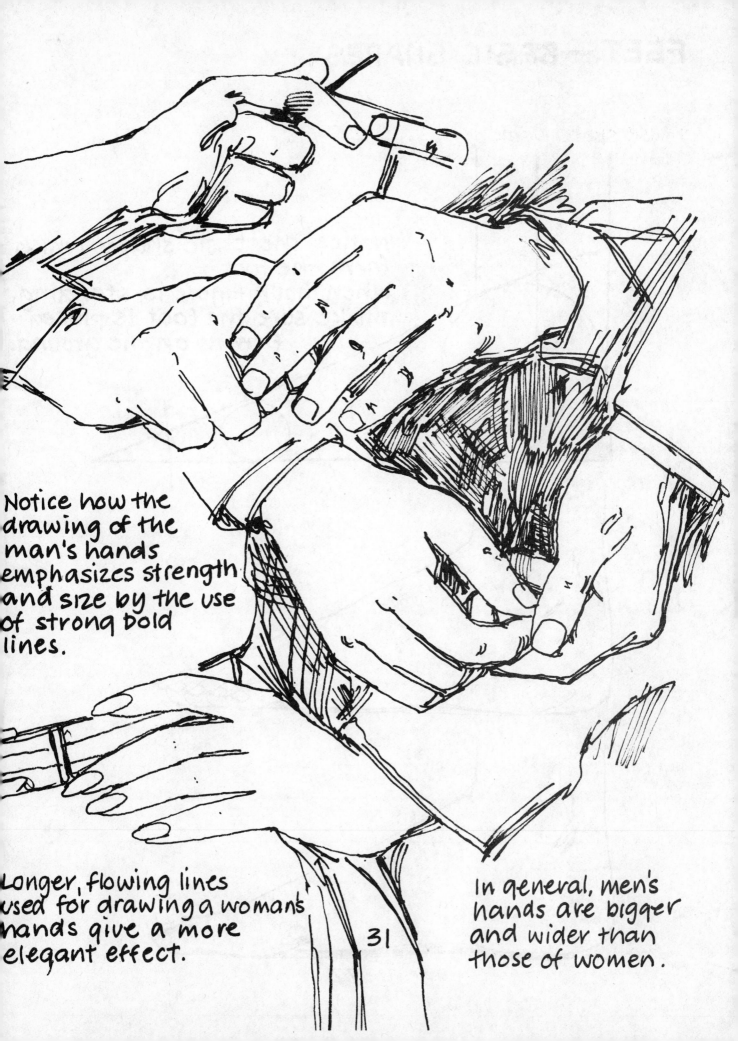

Notice how the drawing of the man's hands emphasizes strength and size by the use of strong bold lines.

Longer, flowing lines used for drawing a woman's hands give a more elegant effect.

In general, men's hands are bigger and wider than those of women.

FEET — BASIC SHAPES

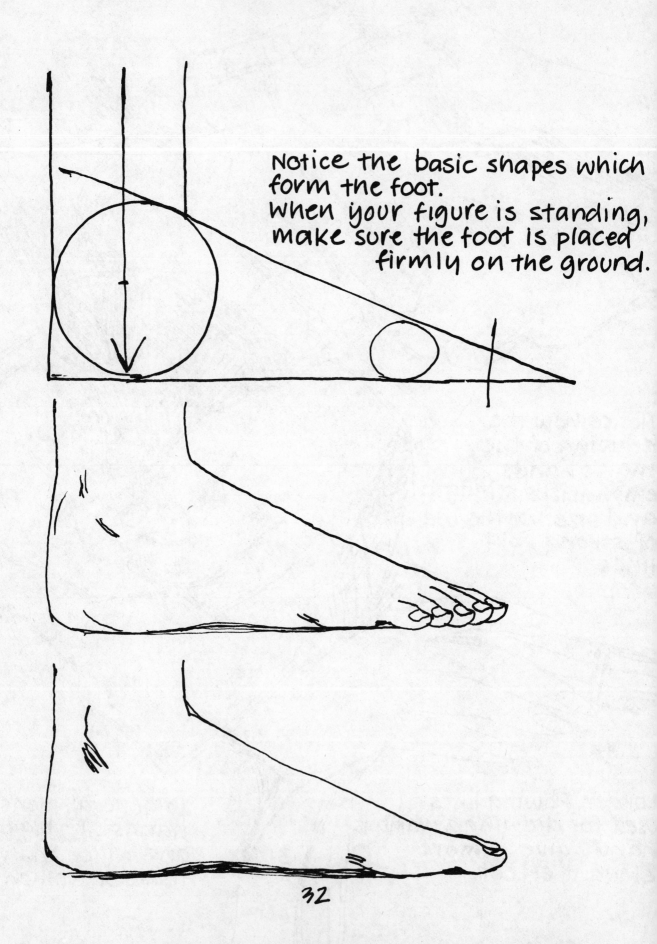

Notice the basic shapes which form the foot.
When your figure is standing, make sure the foot is placed firmly on the ground.

See how different the shape of the foot looks when a person stands with his feet slightly apart. This is known as foreshortening.

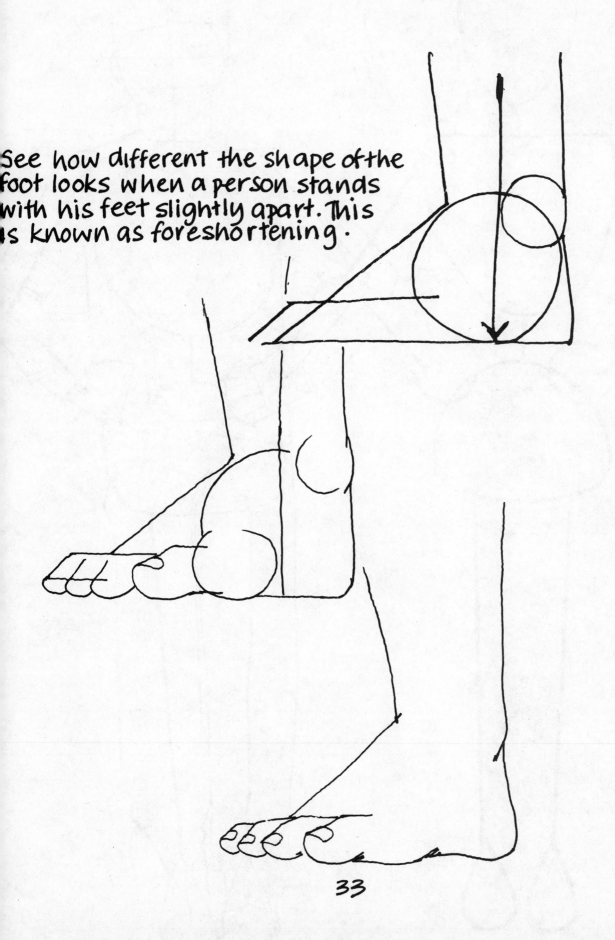

STANDING

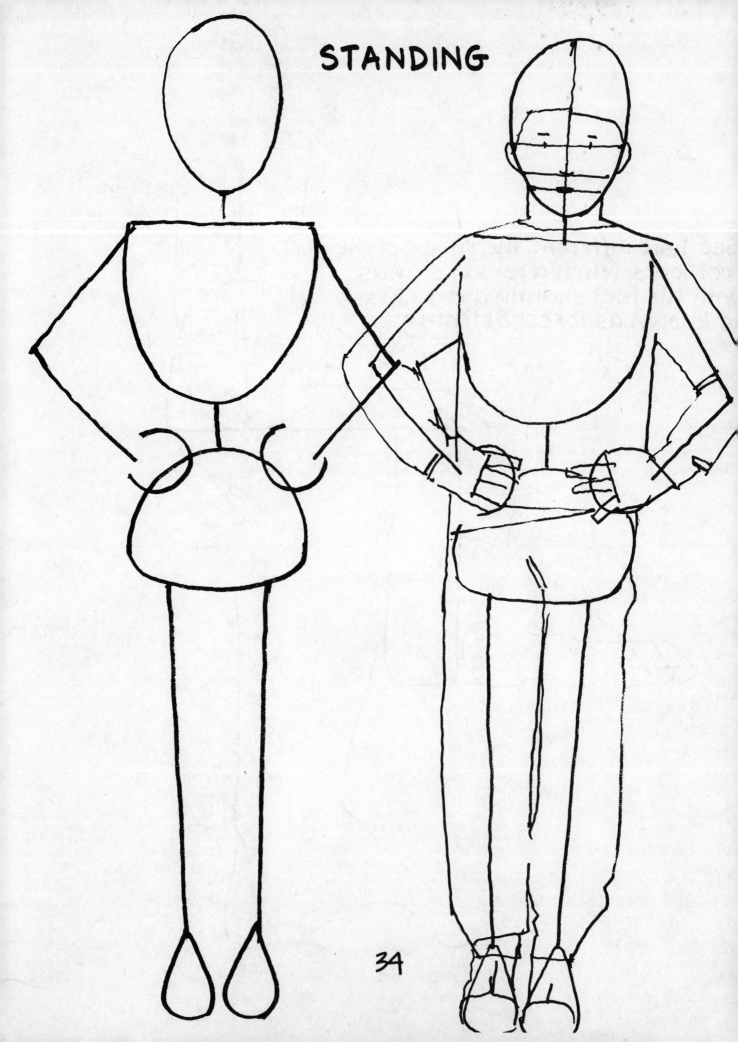

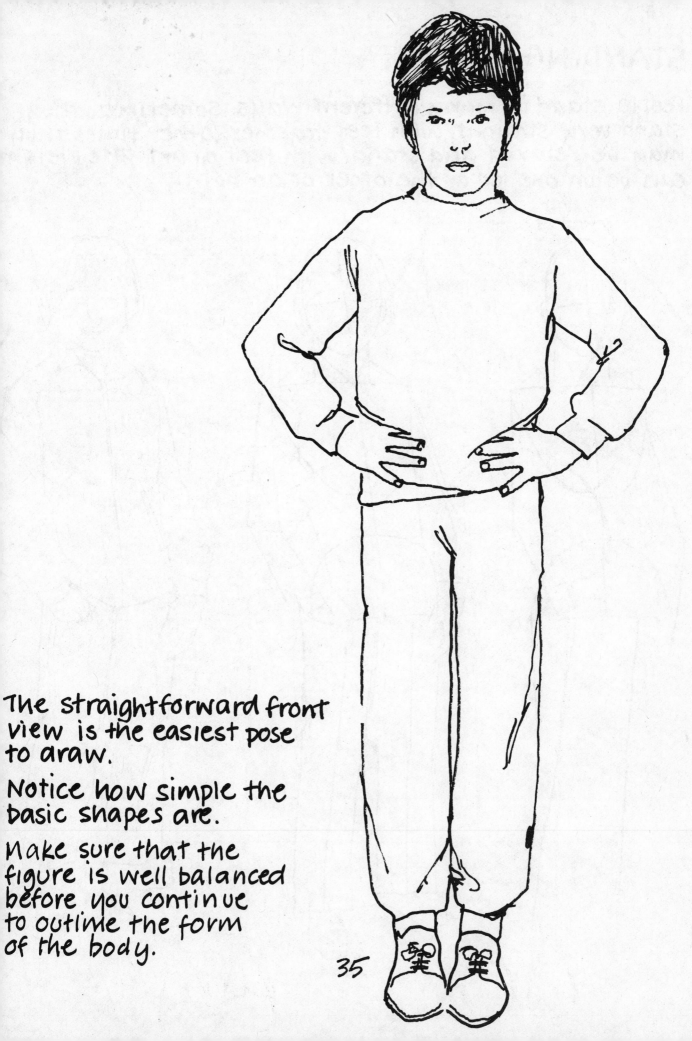

The straightforward front view is the easiest pose to draw.

Notice how simple the basic shapes are.

Make sure that the figure is well balanced before you continue to outline the form of the body.

35

STANDING

People stand in many different ways. Sometimes they stand very straight, with feet together. Other times they may be relaxed and stand with feet apart. The weight can be on one leg or the other or on both.

When sketching the basic lines and forms, remember to balance the figure.

WALKING

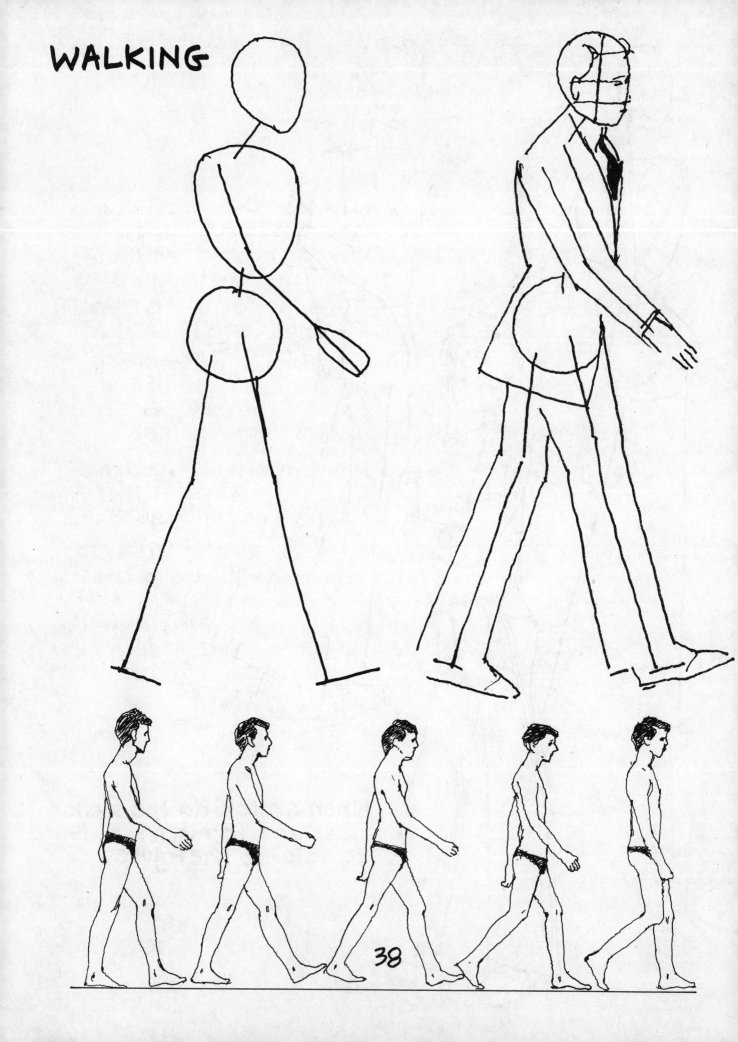

The small drawing across the bottom of this page and others shows the positions the body moves to when walking, running and jumping.

You can see from these how the weight of the body is changed from one foot to the other.

Notice, too, how the arms move to maintain the balance of the figure.

These drawings will help you to understand the movements, and you can use them as a guide when you are posing your action figure.

RUNNING

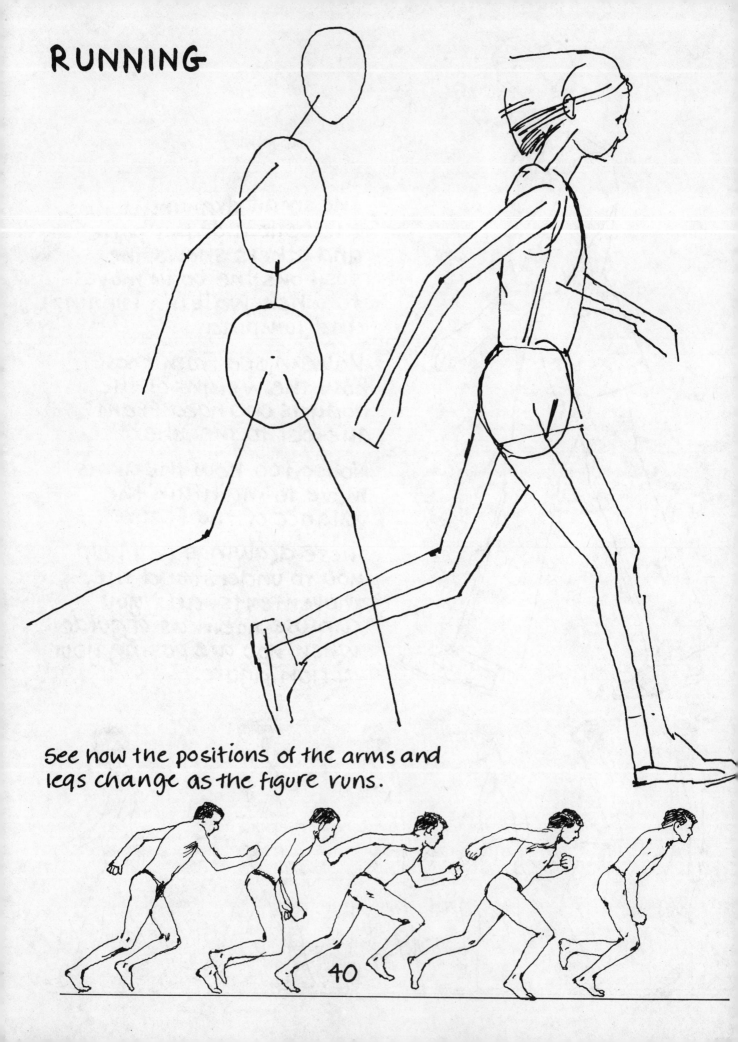

See how the positions of the arms and legs change as the figure runs.

41

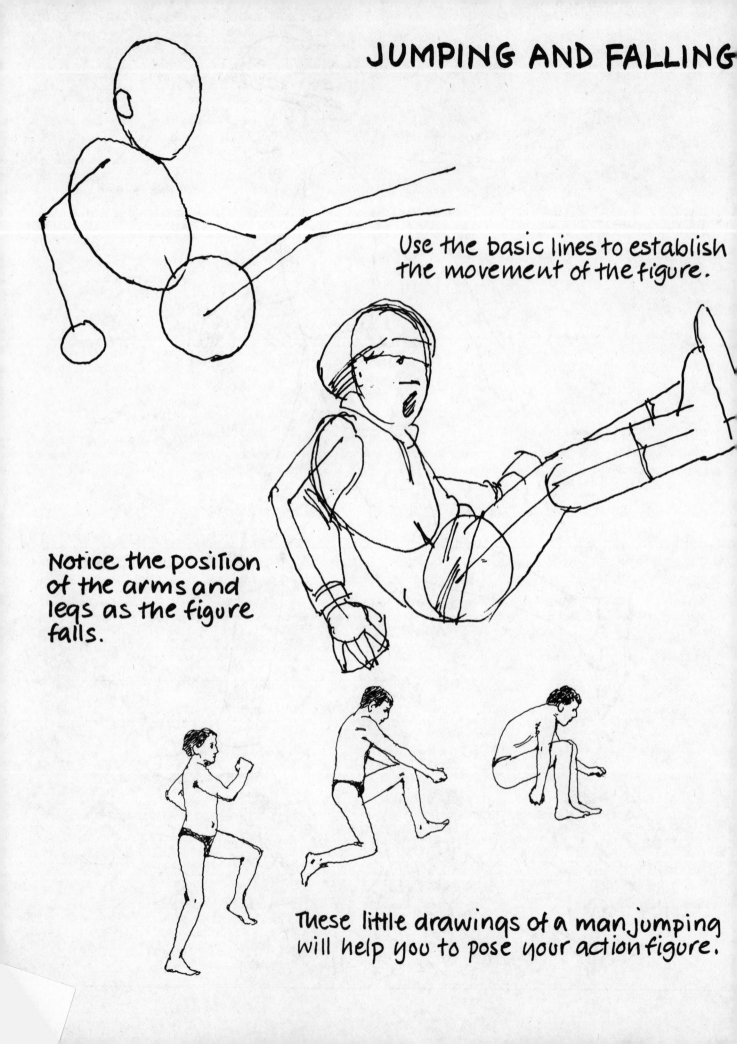

JUMPING AND FALLING

Use the basic lines to establish the movement of the figure.

Notice the position of the arms and legs as the figure falls.

These little drawings of a man jumping will help you to pose your action figure.

Keep your line
free and flowing
to help express
movement.

"Action lines" can
help too.

43

SITTING

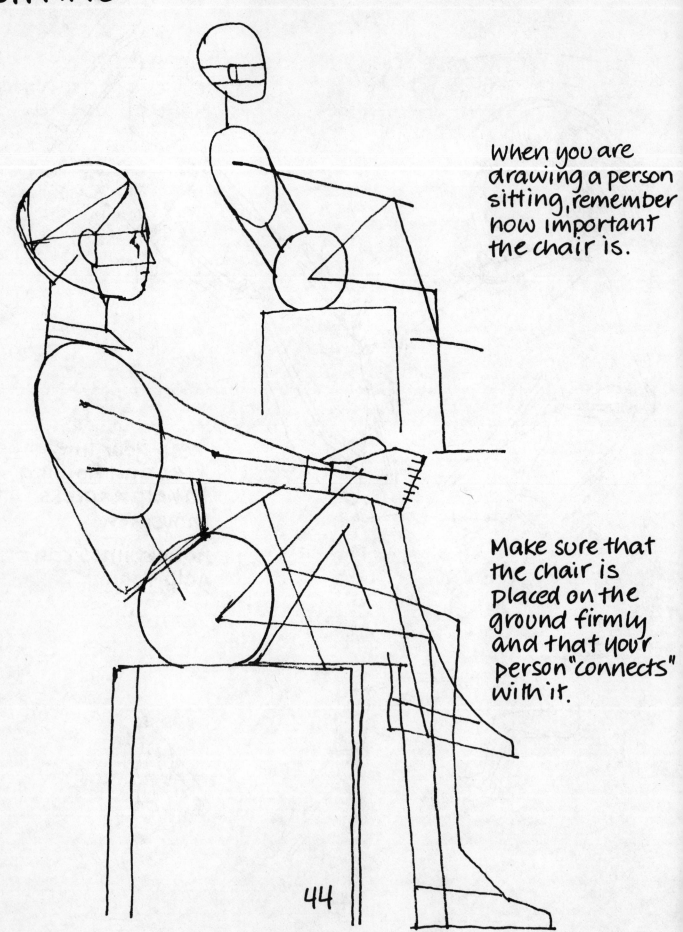

When you are drawing a person sitting, remember how important the chair is.

Make sure that the chair is placed on the ground firmly and that your person "connects" with it.

44

If your friends model for you, they will probably want to sit while you are drawing. You can get lots of practice drawing them in a sitting position. Try to vary your poses as much as possible.

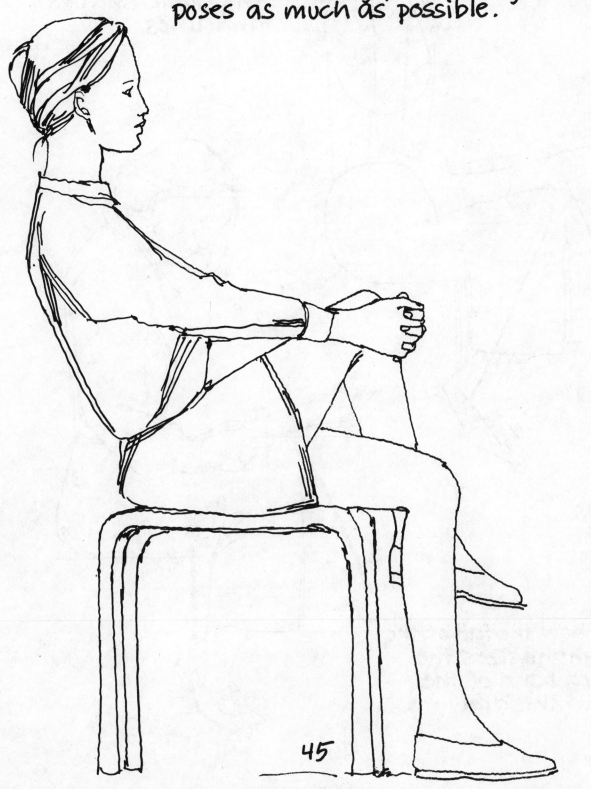

SITTING

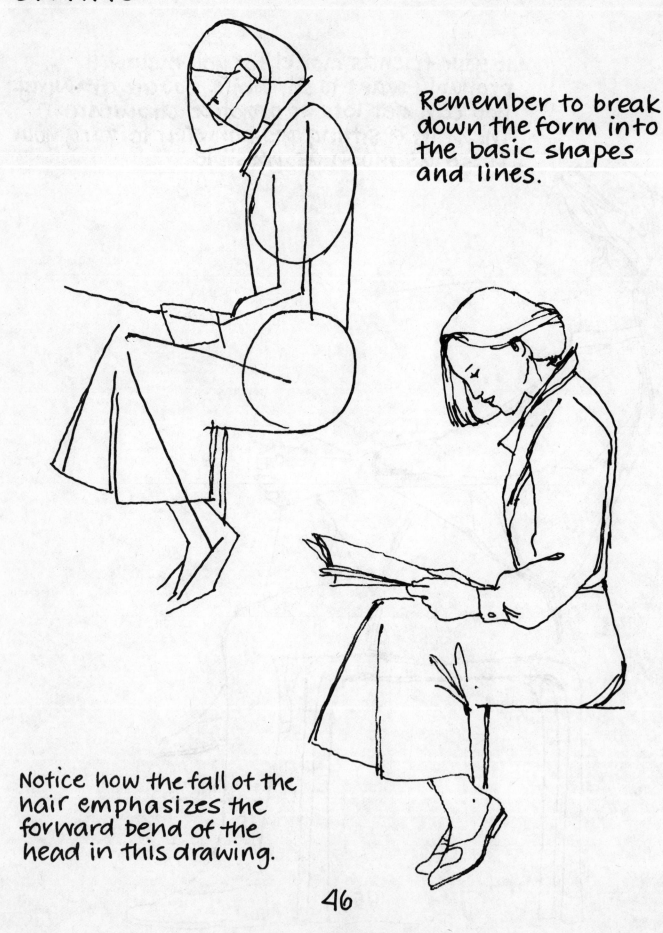

Remember to break down the form into the basic shapes and lines.

Notice how the fall of the hair emphasizes the forward bend of the head in this drawing.

46

Complicated poses can give you a challenge and help you to develop your skills.

47

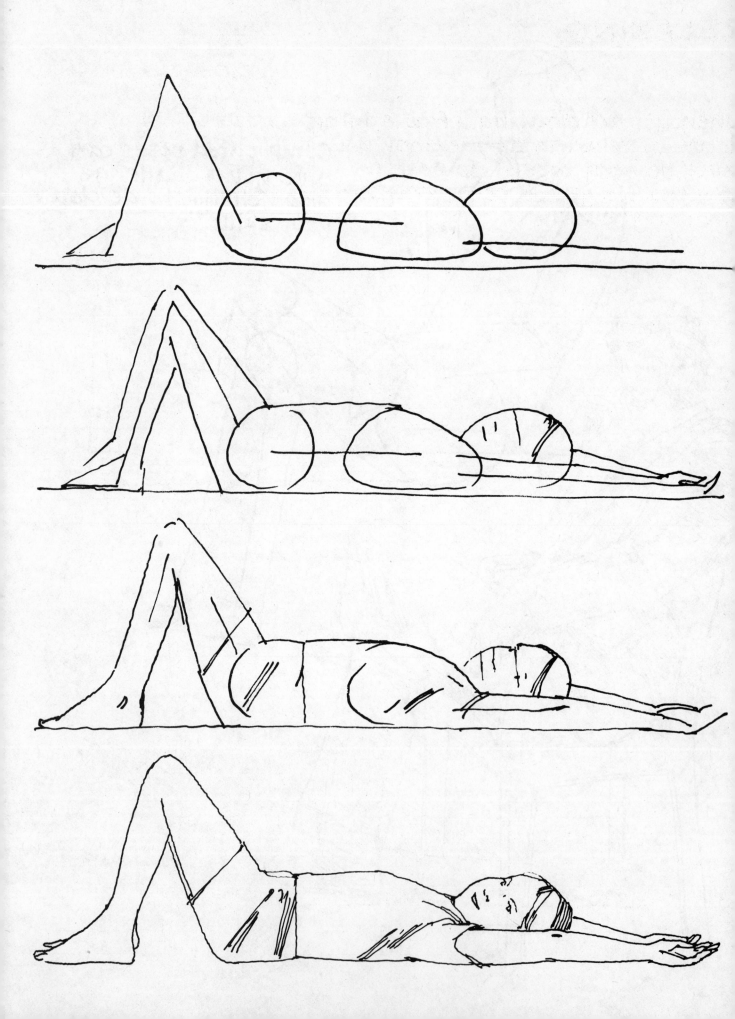

RELAXING

When you are drawing a figure lying down or relaxing on the floor, you must be very careful to notice how the weight is being transferred through the body.

49

BUILD

Humanity is made up of all shapes and sizes. There are thin people, fat people, tall people, short people and those who seem "just right".

You should try to draw as many types of people as possible to develop your skills.

ometimes peoples'
obs determine how
their bodies grow.

he dancer develops
trong legs and
runk while
emaining slim.

he athlete may
develop all his
muscles like the
body builder.

LIFE CLASS

There is no substitute for drawing from life and using real people as your models.

Ask a friend to pose for you and make lots of quick sketches to help you choose a position you like for your drawing. Make sketches of the people you see in your neighborhood.

The drawing below shows you how to use your pencil to help you find the correct proportions of your model. Hold your pencil with your arm out-stretched and measure the length of the head against the pencil. Then see how many times this measurement fits into the rest of the body of your model.

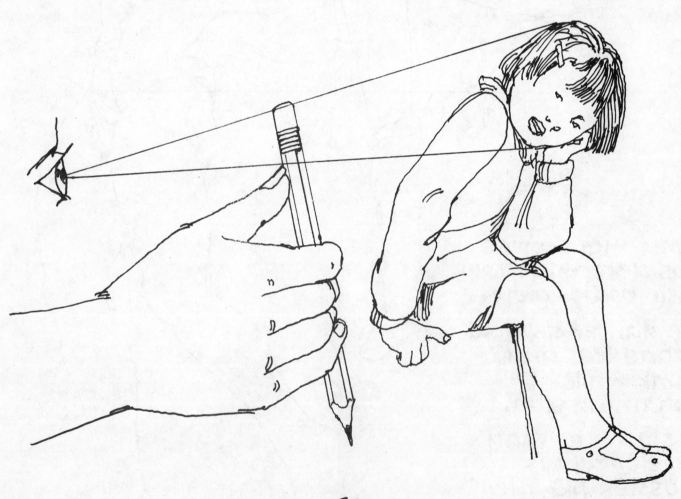

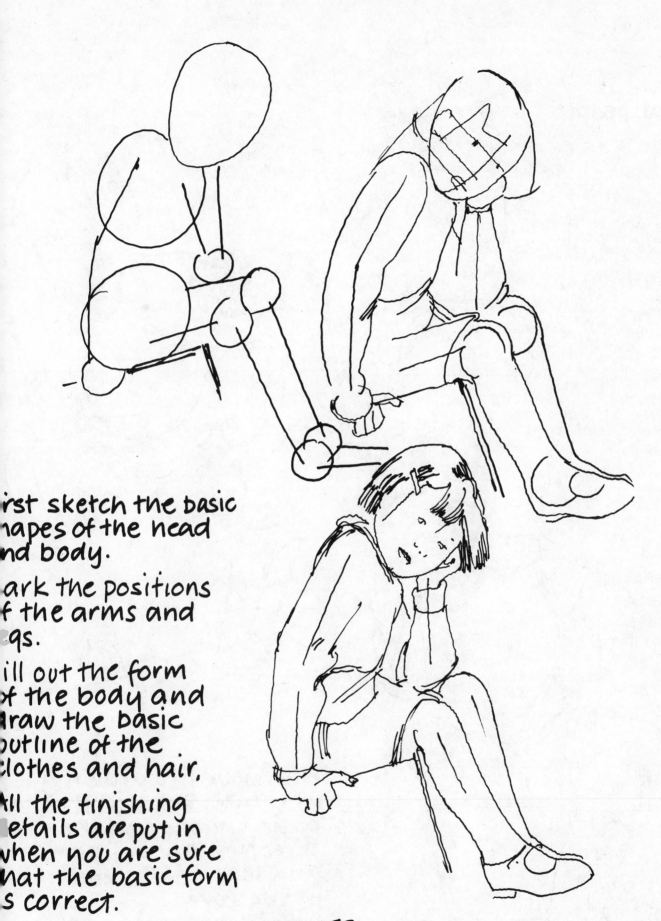

First sketch the basic
shapes of the head
and body.

Mark the positions
of the arms and
legs.

Fill out the form
of the body and
draw the basic
outline of the
clothes and hair.

All the finishing
details are put in
when you are sure
that the basic form
is correct.

53

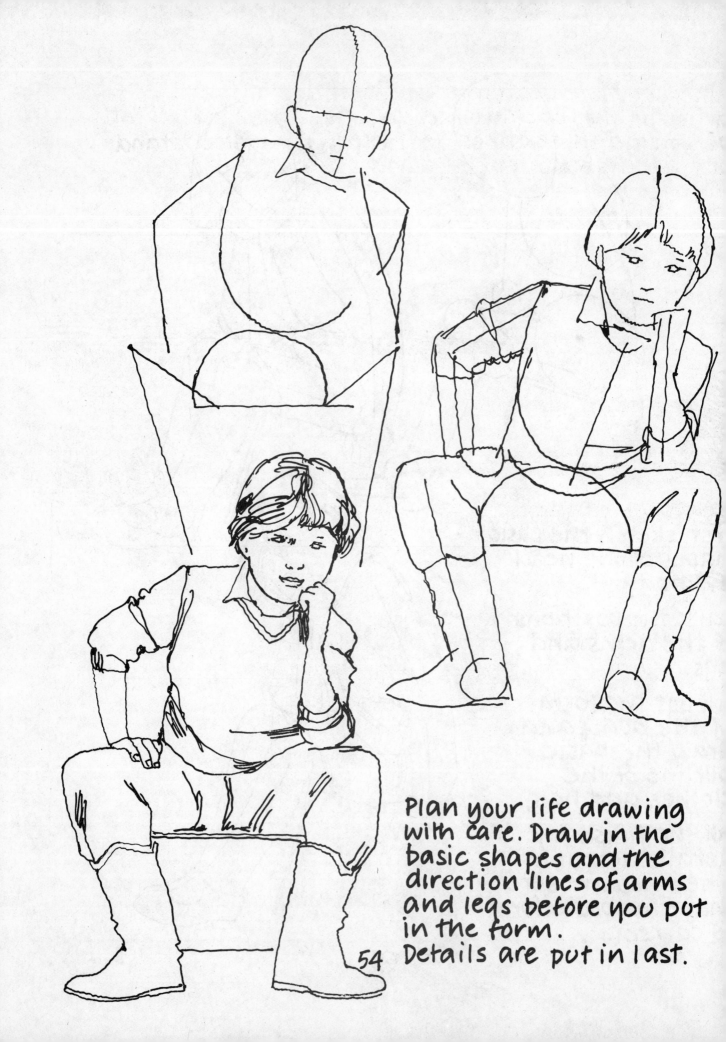

Plan your life drawing
with care. Draw in the
basic shapes and the
direction lines of arms
and legs before you put
in the form.
54 Details are put in last.

when you are drawing from life you might like to draw in the background also. Try to use a variety of lines and textures to help your model stand out against the background.

Carry a sketch book with you
when you go out and draw
the people you see
around you in
your neighborhood.

HOW TO MAKE THE ACTION FIGURE

All the pieces you need to make the action figure are on the back page of this book. If you don't want to spoil your book trace the shapes and paste them onto thin cardboard. Be sure to mark all the dots and letters in the correct places.

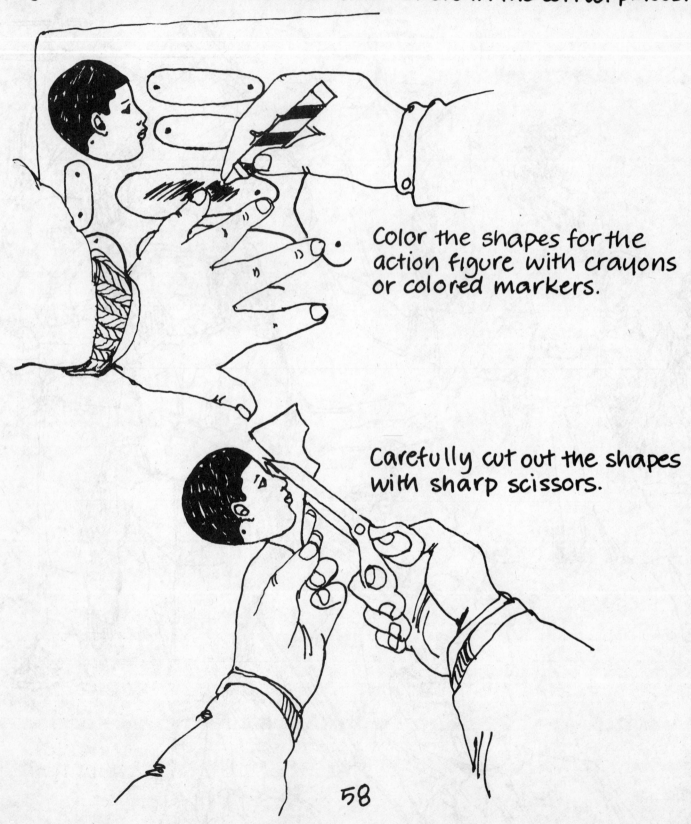

Color the shapes for the action figure with crayons or colored markers.

Carefully cut out the shapes with sharp scissors.

Make holes through all the dots with a sharp needle.

Take care! Don't hurt yourself.

Match the dots by their letters and join them together with paper fasteners.

Be sure to put all the correct dots together.

Adjust the paper fasteners so that the pieces of the action figure will move freely without being too loose.

Now you can pose your action figure and use it as a model. The next page will show you how to do this.

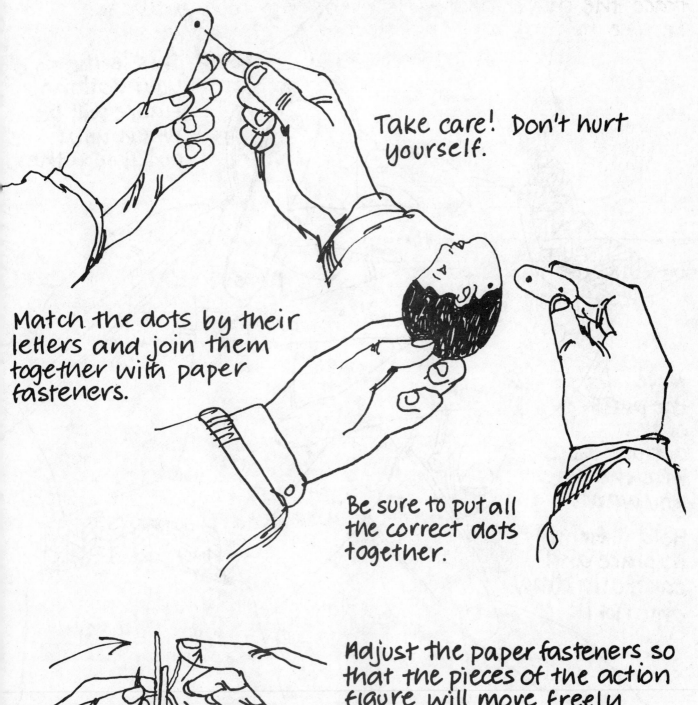

HOW TO USE THE ACTION FIGURE

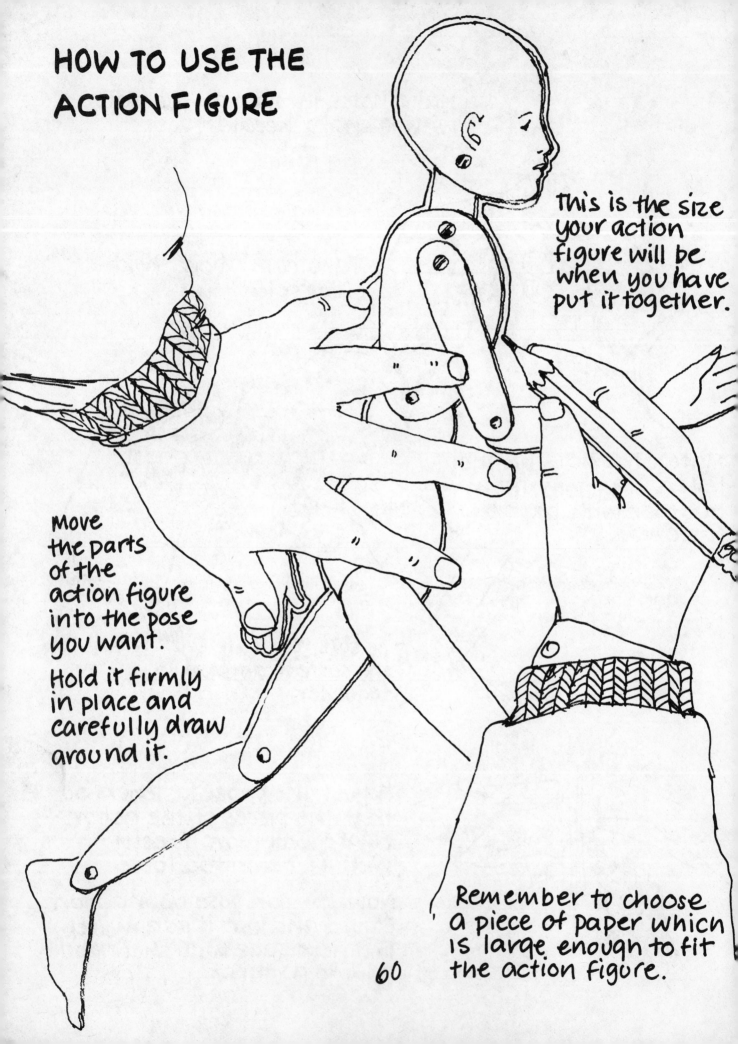

This is the size your action figure will be when you have put it together.

Move the parts of the action figure into the pose you want.

Hold it firmly in place and carefully draw around it.

60

Remember to choose a piece of paper which is large enough to fit the action figure.

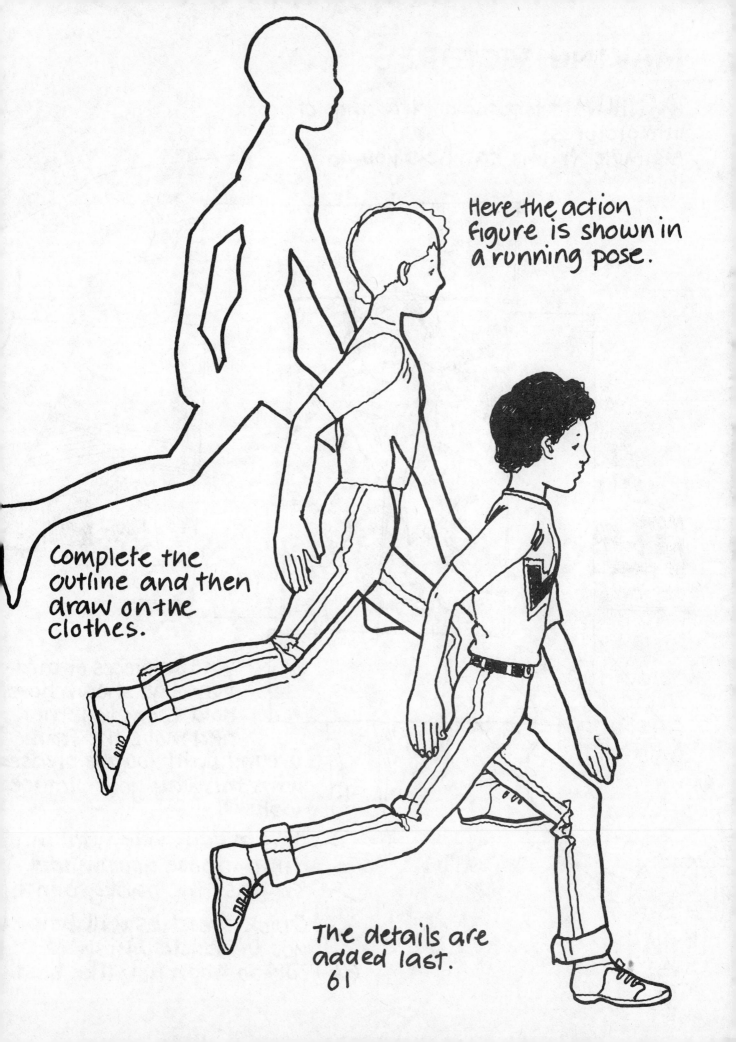

Here the action figure is shown in a running pose.

Complete the outline and then draw on the clothes.

The details are added last.

61

MAKING PICTURES.

You will want to put your drawings of people into pictures.
A simple "frame" can help you do this.

Cut two pieces of cardboard as shown here. Hold them together and move the frame around until you are pleased with the way your picture looks.

It is always worth taking time to pose your model against the background.

Quick sketches will help you to decide which composition you like best.

62